GOSPEL FAVORITES
FOR UKULELE

ISBN 978-1-4950-8852-0

HAL•LEONARD®

7777 W. BLUEMOUND RD. P.O. BOX 13819 MILWAUKEE, WI 53213

Visit Hal Leonard Online at
www.halleonard.com

Because He Lives

Words and Music by William J. Gaither and Gloria Gaither

First note

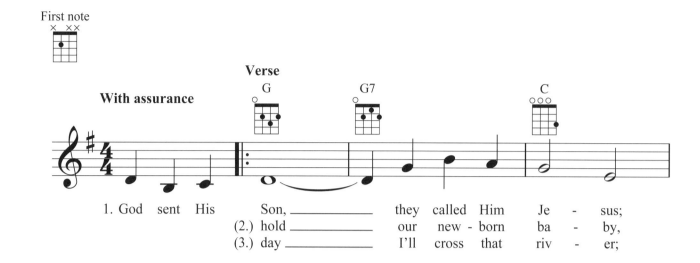

Verse

With assurance

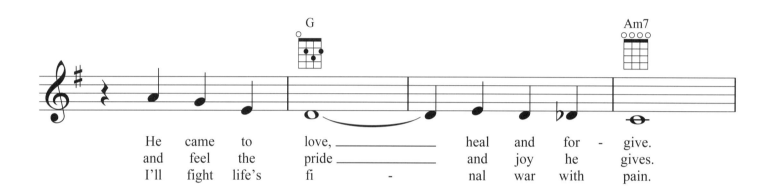

1. God sent His Son, _____ they called Him Je - sus;
(2.) hold _____ our new - born ba - by,
(3.) day _____ I'll cross that riv - er;

He came to love, _____ heal and for - give.
and feel the pride _____ and joy he gives.
I'll fight life's fi - nal war with pain.

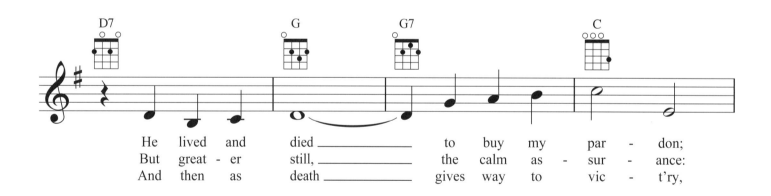

He lived and died _____ to buy my par - don;
But great - er still, _____ the calm as - sur - ance:
And then as death _____ gives way to vic - t'ry,

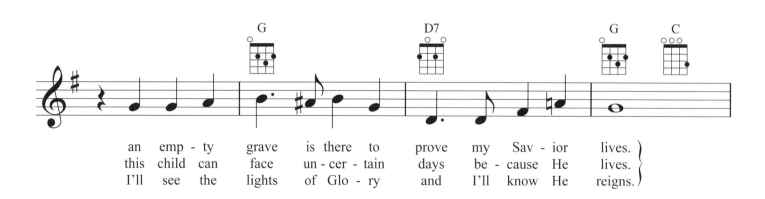

an emp - ty grave is there to prove my Sav - ior lives.
this child can face un - cer - tain days be - cause He lives.
I'll see the lights of Glo - ry and I'll know He reigns.

Chorus

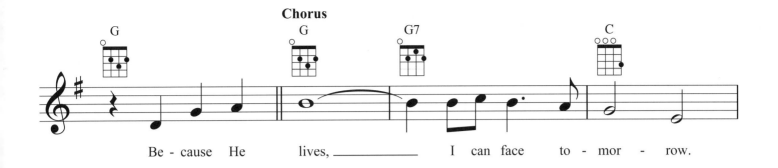

Be - cause He lives, _____ I can face to - mor - row.

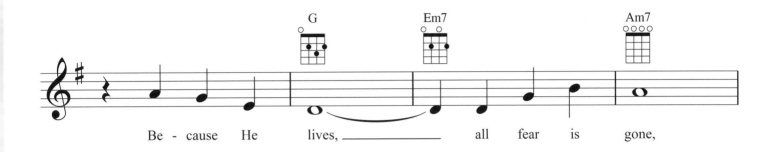

Be - cause He lives, _____ all fear is gone,

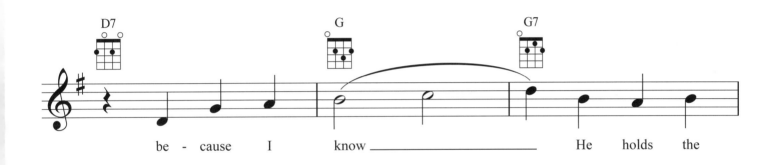

be - cause I know _____ He holds the

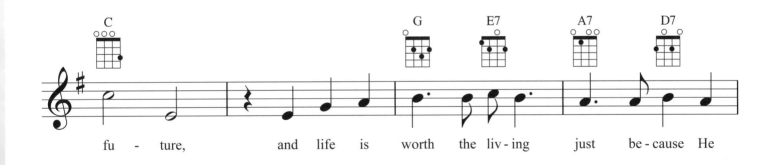

fu - ture, and life is worth the liv - ing just be - cause He

1., 2.

lives.

2. How sweet to
3. And then one

3.

lives. _____

Daddy Sang Bass

Words and Music by Carl Perkins

First note

Verse

Moderately, in 2

1. I re - mem-ber when I was a lad, times were hard and things were
(2.) mem - ber af - ter work, Ma - ma would call in all of

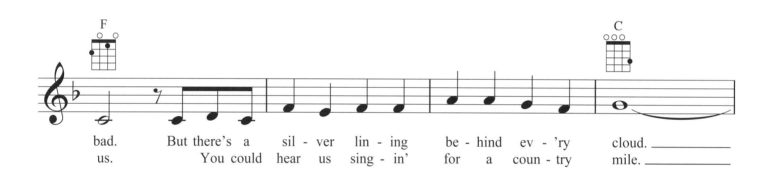

bad. But there's a sil - ver lin - ing be - hind ev - 'ry cloud. _____
us. You could hear us sing - in' for a coun - try mile. _____

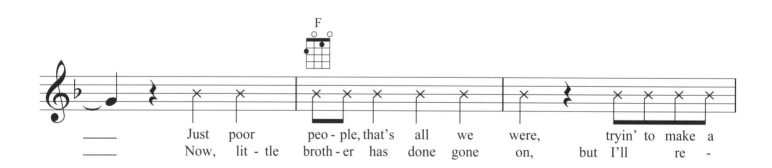

_____ Just poor peo - ple, that's all we were, tryin' to make a
_____ Now, lit - tle broth - er has done gone on, but I'll re -

liv - in' out of black land dirt. But we'd get to - geth - er in a fam - 'ly
join him in a song. We'll be to - geth - er a - gain _____ up

I Believe

Words and Music by Ervin Drake, Irvin Graham, Jimmy Shirl and Al Stillman

He Touched Me

Words and Music by William J. Gaither

First note

Verse
Moderately

1. Shack - led by a heav - y bur - den, _____
2. Since I met this bless - ed Sav - ior, _____

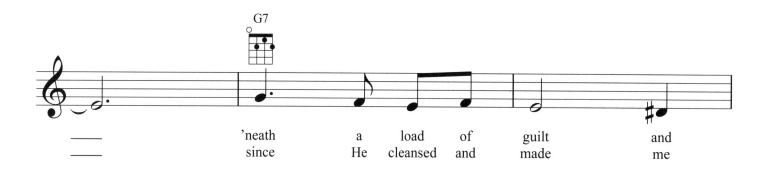

_____ 'neath a load of guilt and
_____ since He cleansed and made me

shame. _____ Then the hand of Je - sus
whole, _____ I will nev - er cease to

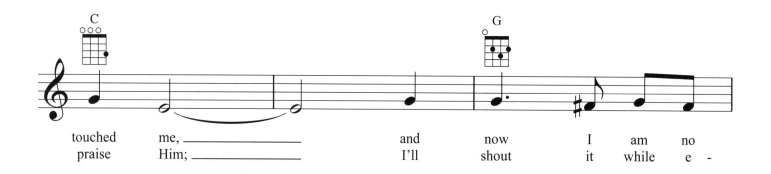

touched me, _____ and now I am no
praise Him; _____ I'll shout it while e -

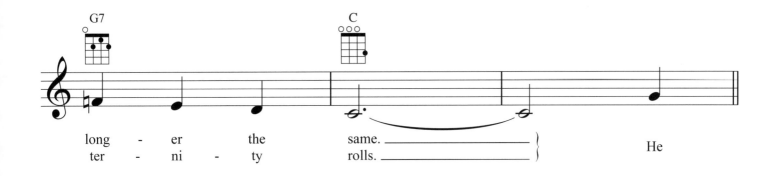

long - er the same. _____
ter - ni - ty rolls. _____
He

Chorus

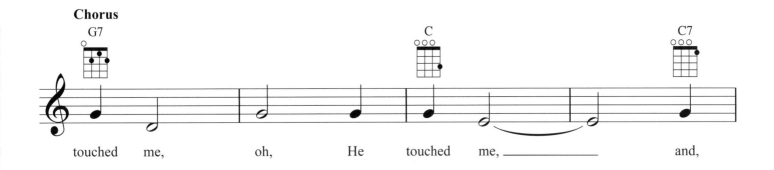

touched me, oh, He touched me, _____ and,

oh, the joy that floods my soul. _____

Some - thing ___ hap - pened ___ and now I know He

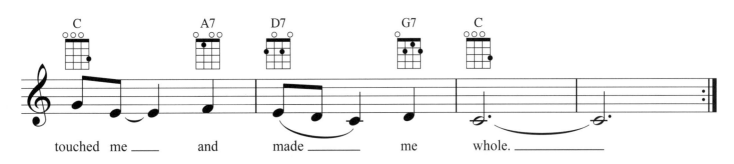

touched me ___ and made ___ me whole. _____

How Great Thou Art

Words by Stuart K. Hine
Swedish Folk Melody Adapted and Arranged by Stuart K. Hine

Author's original lyrics are "works" and "mighty."

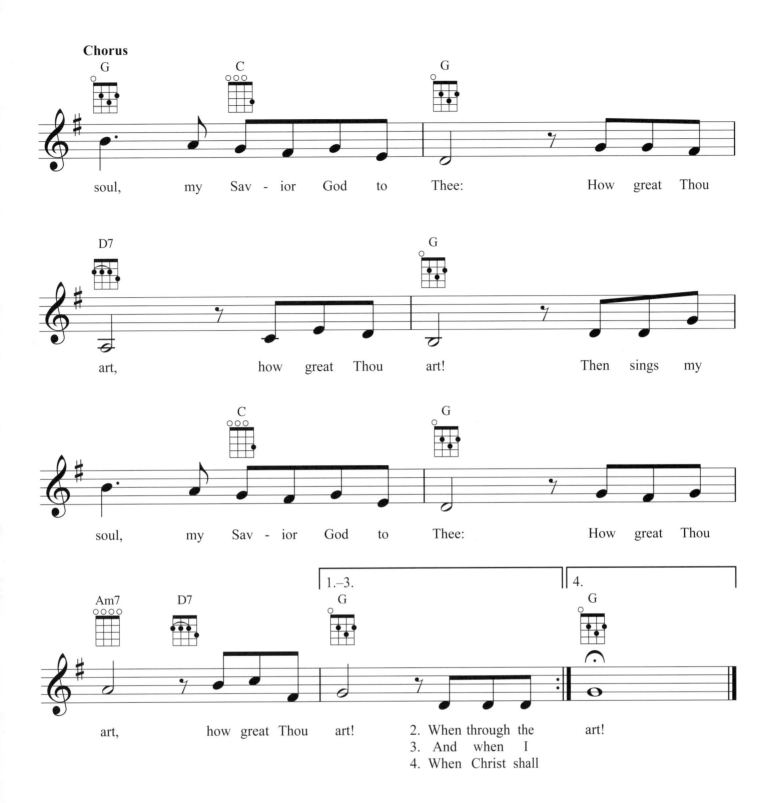

Additional Lyrics

3. And when I think, that God, His Son not sparing,
   Sent Him to die, I scarce can take it in;
   That on the cross, my burden gladly bearing,
   He bled and died to take away my sin.

4. When Christ shall come with shout of acclamation
   And take me home, what joy shall fill my heart!
   Then I shall bow in humble adoration
   And there proclaim: My God, how great Thou art!

I Saw the Light

Words and Music by Hank Williams

First note

Verse

Lively, in 2

1. I wan - dered so aim - less, life filled with
2., 3. *See additional lyrics*

sin. I would - n't let my dear Sav - ior in.

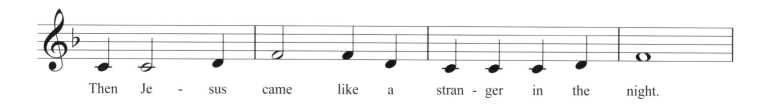

Then Je - sus came like a stran - ger in the night.

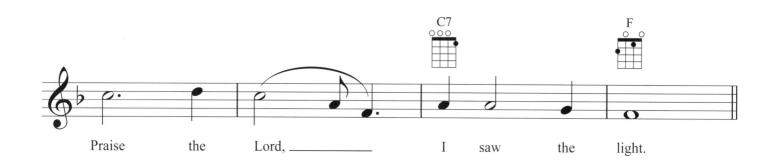

Praise the Lord, _____ I saw the light.

Chorus

I saw the light, _____ I saw the light, _____

no more _____ dark - ness, no more night. _____ Now I'm so

hap - py, no sor - row in sight. _____ Praise the Lord, _____

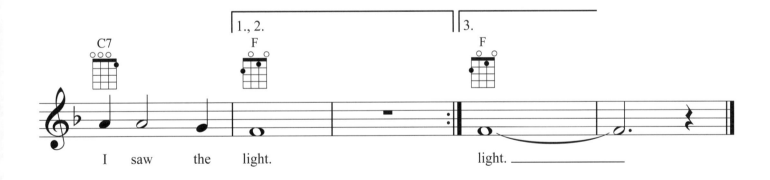

1., 2.

3.

I saw the light.   light. _____

Additional Lyrics

2. Just like a blind man I wandered along,
   Worries and fears I claimed for my own.
   Then like the blind man that God gave back his sight,
   Praise the Lord, I saw the light.

3. I was a fool to wander and stray,
   Straight is the gate and narrow is the way.
   Now I have traded the wrong for the right.
   Praise the Lord, I saw the light.

I'd Rather Have Jesus

Words by Rhea F. Miller
Music by George Beverly Shea

First note

Thoughtfully

Verse

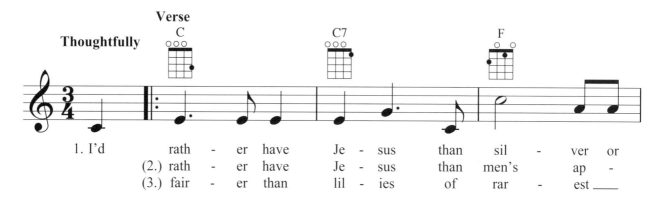

1. I'd rath - er have Je - sus than sil - ver or
(2.) rath - er have Je - sus than men's ap -
(3.) fair - er than lil - ies of rar - est ___

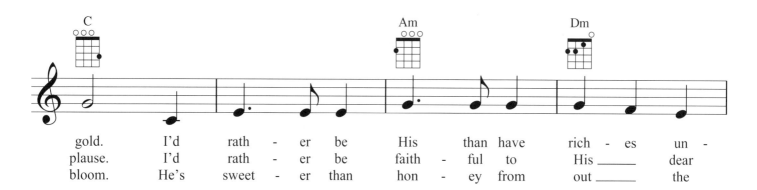

gold. I'd rath - er be His than have rich - es un -
plause. I'd rath - er be faith - ful to His ___ dear
bloom. He's sweet - er than hon - ey from out ___ the

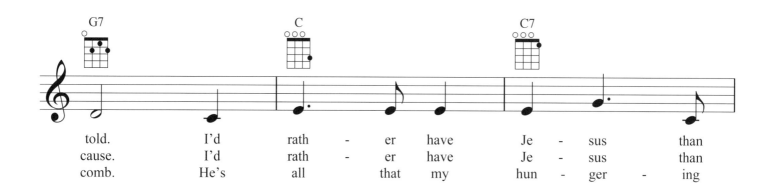

told. I'd rath - er have Je - sus than
cause. I'd rath - er have Je - sus than
comb. He's all that my hun - ger - ing

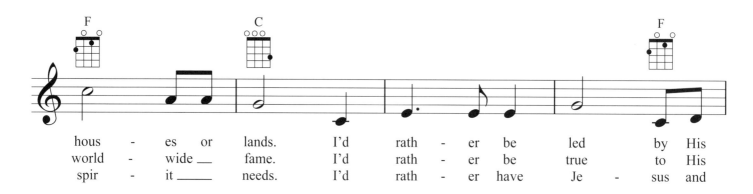

hous - es or lands. I'd rath - er be led by His
world - wide ___ fame. I'd rath - er be true to His
spir - it ___ needs. I'd rath - er have Je - sus and

Chorus

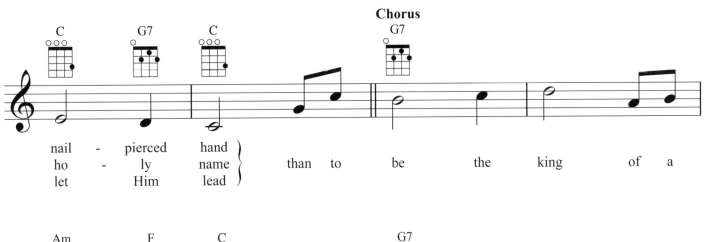

nail - pierced hand
ho - ly name } than to be the king of a
let Him lead

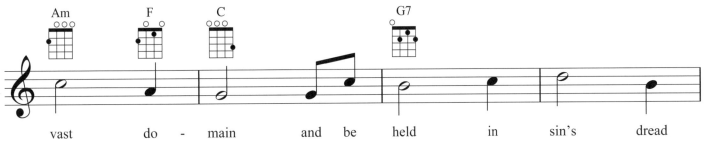

vast do - main and be held in sin's dread

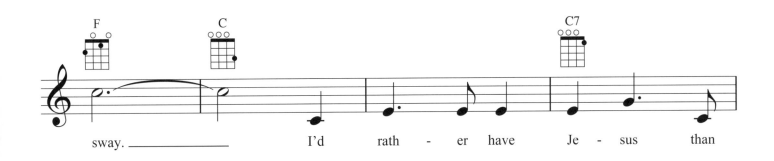

sway. _____ I'd rath - er have Je - sus than

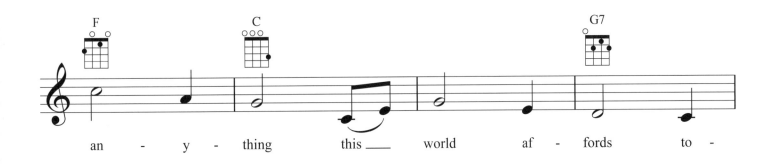

an - y - thing this __ world af - fords to -

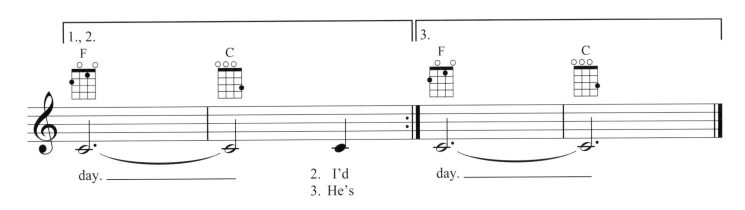

day. _____ 2. I'd day. _____

3. He's

I'll Fly Away

Words and Music by Albert E. Brumley

First note

Verse
Brightly, in 2

1. Some bright morn - ing when this life is
2. When the shad - ows of this life have
3. Oh, how glad and hap - py when we
4. Just a few more wea - ry days and

o'er, I'll _____ fly a - way,
gone, I'll _____ fly a - way,
meet, I'll _____ fly a - way,
then, I'll _____ fly a - way,

to that home on God's ce - les - tial shore,
like a bird from pris - on bars has flown,
no more cold i-ron shack - les on my feet.
to a land where joys will nev - er end,

I'll _____ fly a - way.

Chorus

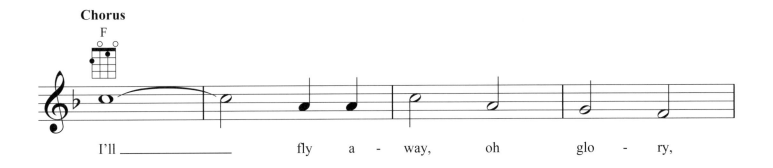

I'll _____ fly a - way, oh glo - ry,

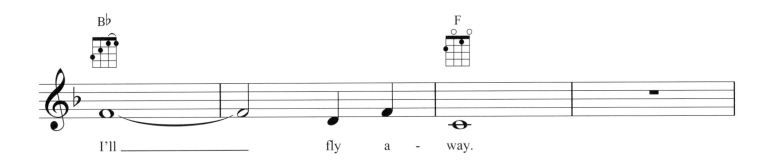

I'll _____ fly a - way.

When I die, hal - le - lu - jah, by and

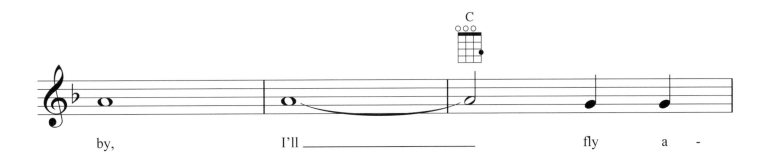

by, I'll _____ fly a -

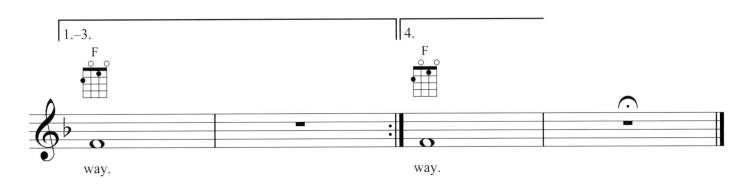

way. way.

The King Is Coming

Words by William J. and Gloria Gaither and Charles Millhuff
Music by William J. Gaither

First note

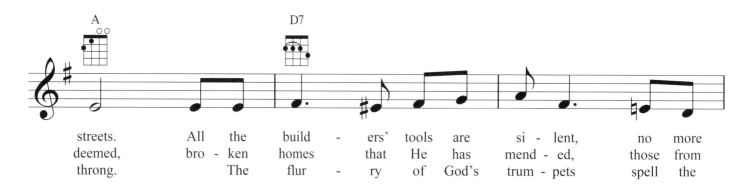

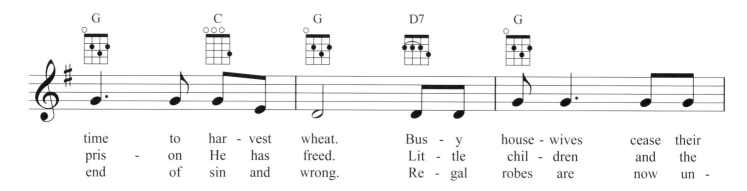

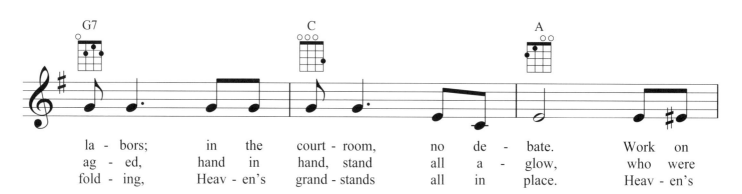

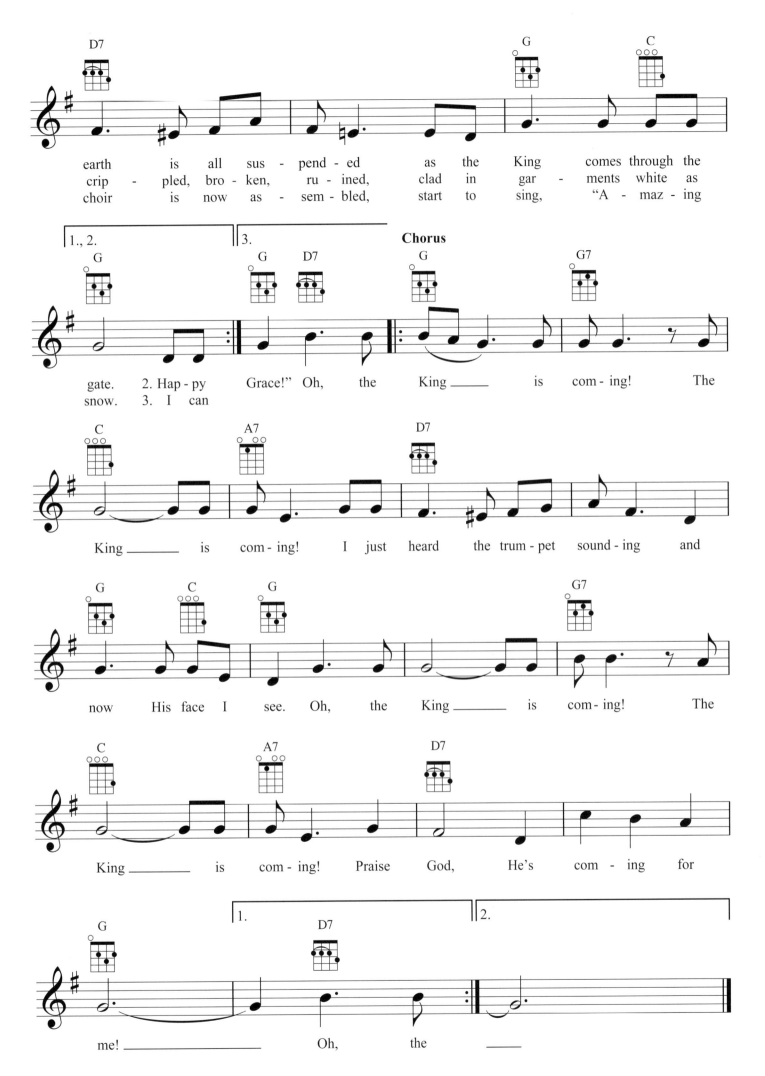

earth   is   all   sus - pend - ed   as   the   King   comes through the
crip - pled, bro - ken,   ru - ined,   clad   in   gar - ments white as
choir   is   now   as - sem - bled,   start   to   sing,   "A - maz - ing

1., 2. | **3.** | **Chorus**

gate. 2. Hap - py   Grace!" Oh,   the   King _____ is com - ing!   The
snow. 3. I can

King _____ is com - ing!   I   just   heard   the trum - pet   sound - ing   and

now   His face   I   see.   Oh,   the   King _____ is   com - ing!   The

King _____ is   com - ing!   Praise   God,   He's   com - ing   for

1. | **2.**

me! _____   Oh,   the   _____

Learning to Lean

Words and Music by John Stallings

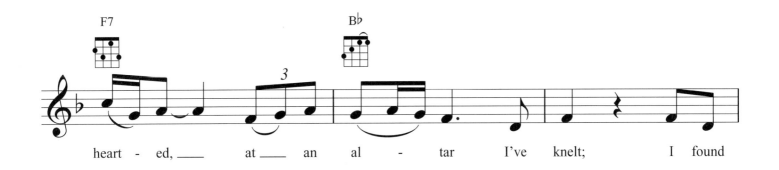

heart - ed, _____ at _____ an al - tar I've knelt; I found

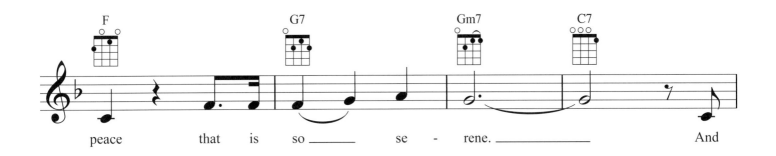

peace that is so _____ se - rene. _____ And

all that He asks _____ is _____ a child - like

trust and a heart that is learn - ing to _____

Coda

D.C. al Coda
(with repeat)

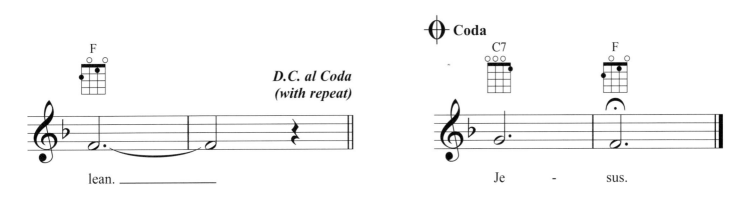

lean. _____   Je - sus.

The Longer I Serve Him

Words and Music by William J. Gaither

Chorus

grows. _____ The long - er I serve Him, the

sweet - er He grows. _____ The more that I

love Him, more love He be - stows. Each

day is like heav - en; my heart o - ver -

flows. The long - er I serve ___ Him, the

sweet - er He grows.   grows.

Mansion Over the Hilltop

Words and Music by Ira F. Stanphill

My God Is Real
(Yes, God Is Real)
Words and Music by Kenneth Morris

My Tribute

Words and Music by Andraé Crouch

Precious Lord, Take My Hand
(Take My Hand, Precious Lord)

Words and Music by Thomas A. Dorsey

1. Pre - cious Lord, take my hand, lead me on, help me stand. __ I am
(2., 3.) *See additional lyrics*

tired, I am weak, I am worn. _____ Through the storm, through the

night, lead me on to the light. __ Take my hand, __ pre - cious

Lord; __ lead me home. _____ 2. When my home. _____
2. When my
3. When the

Additional Lyrics

2. When my way grows drear, precious Lord, linger near
   When my life is almost gone.
   Hear my cry, hear my call, hold my hand lest I fall.
   Take my hand, precious Lord; lead me home.

3. When the darkness appears and the night draws near,
   And the day is past and gone,
   At the river I stand; guide my feet, hold my hand.
   Take my hand, precious Lord; lead me home.

There's Something About That Name

Words by William J. and Gloria Gaither
Music by William J. Gaither

Put Your Hand in the Hand

Words and Music by Gene MacLellan

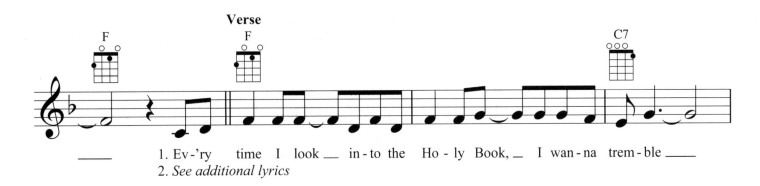

1. Ev-'ry time I look __ in-to the Ho-ly Book, __ I wan-na trem-ble ____
2. *See additional lyrics*

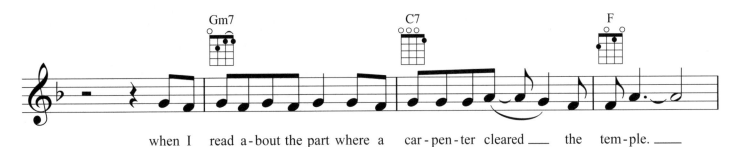

when I read a-bout the part where a car-pen-ter cleared __ the tem-ple. ____

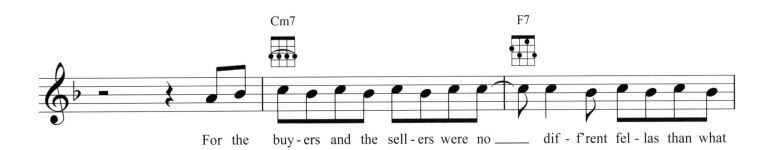

For the buy-ers and the sell-ers were no _____ dif-f'rent fel-las than what

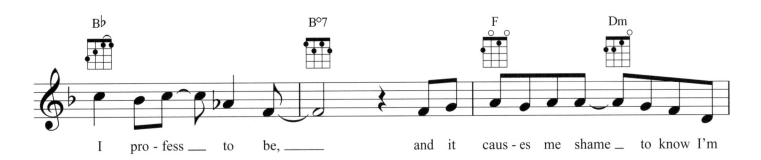

I pro-fess __ to be, _____ and it caus-es me shame __ to know I'm

2nd time, D.S. al Coda   **Coda**

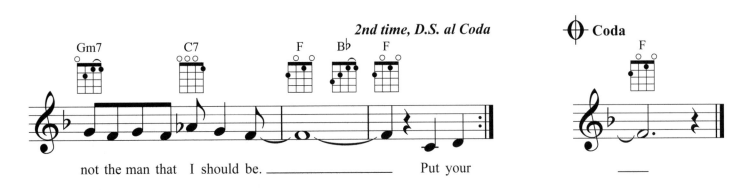

not the man that I should be. _____ Put your   ____

Additional Lyrics

2. Mama taught me how to pray before I reached the age of seven.
When I'm down on my knees, that's a-when I'm close to heaven.
Daddy lived his life with two kids and a wife, and he did what he could do.
And he showed me enough of what it takes to get you through.

Soon and Very Soon

Words and Music by Andraé Crouch

First note

Verse
Soulfully, in 2

1. Soon and ver - y soon, _____ we are
2. No more cry - in' there, _____ we are
3. No more dy - in' there, _____ we are

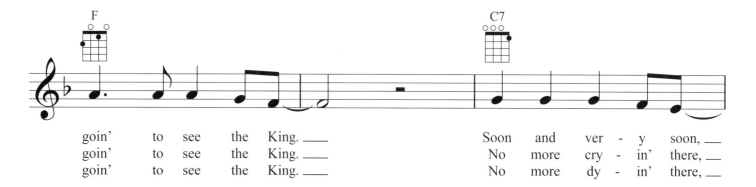

goin' to see the King. _____   Soon and ver - y soon, ___
goin' to see the King. _____   No more cry - in' there, ___
goin' to see the King. _____   No more dy - in' there, ___

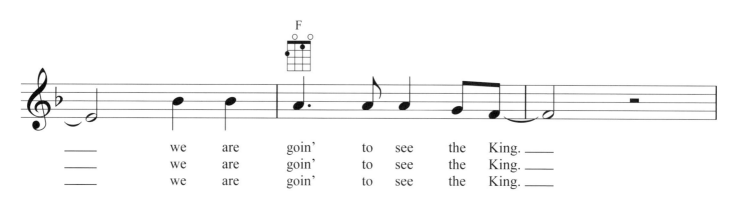

_____ we are goin' to see the King. _____
_____ we are goin' to see the King. _____
_____ we are goin' to see the King. _____

Soon and ver - y soon, ___ }
No more cry - in' there, ___ }   we are goin' to see the King. ___
No more dy - in' there, ___ }

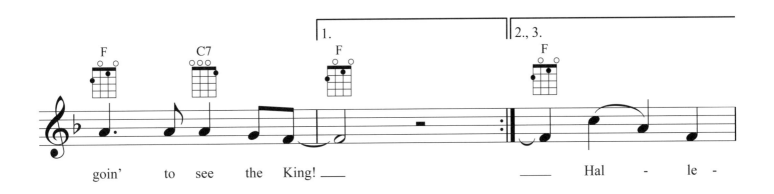

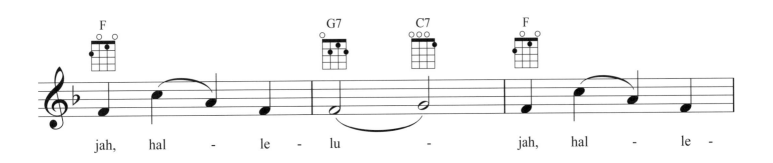

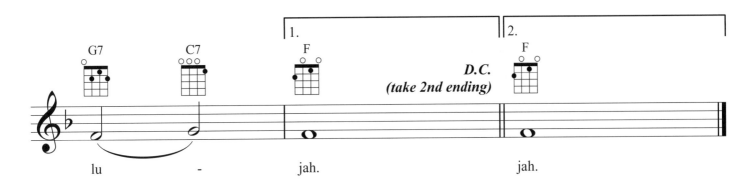

Turn Your Radio On

Words and Music by Albert E. Brumley

on, _____ }
God, _____ }
turn your ra - di - o on. Turn your ra - di - o

Chorus

on _____ and lis - ten to the mu - sic in the

air. Turn your ra - di - o on, _____ heav - en's glo - ry share.

Turn your lights down low _____ and lis - ten to the Mas - ter's ra - di -

1.
o. Get in touch with God, _____ turn your ra - di - o on.

2.
2. Don't you know that ev - 'ry - on. _____

Victory in Jesus

Words and Music by E.M. Bartlett

First note

Verse

Joyfully

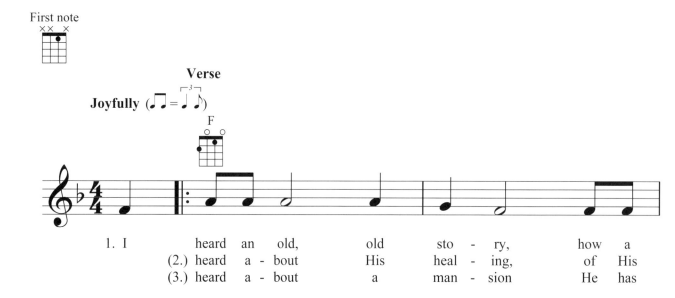

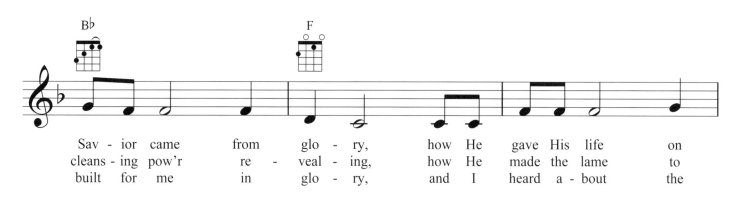

1. I   heard an old,   old   sto - ry,   how a
(2.) heard a - bout   His   heal - ing,   of His
(3.) heard a - bout   a   man - sion   He has

Sav - ior came   from   glo - ry,   how He gave His life   on
cleans - ing pow'r   re -   veal - ing,   how He made the lame   to
built for me   in   glo - ry,   and I heard a - bout   the

Cal - va - ry   to   save a wretch   like   me.   I
walk a - gain   and   caused the blind   to   see.   And
streets of gold   be -   yond the crys -   tal   sea,   a -

heard a - bout   His   groan - ing,   of His   pre - cious blood's   a -
then I cried,   "Dear   Je - sus,   come and   heal my bro - ken
bout the an - gels   sing - ing,   and the   old re - demp - tion

Ride the Ukulele Wave!

The Beach Boys for Ukulele

This folio features 20 favorites, including: Barbara Ann • Be True to Your School • California Girls • Fun, Fun, Fun • God Only Knows • Good Vibrations • Help Me Rhonda • I Get Around • In My Room • Kokomo • Little Deuce Coupe • Sloop John B • Surfin' U.S.A. • Wouldn't It Be Nice • and more!

00701726 . . . .$14.99

Disney Songs for Ukulele

20 great Disney classics arranged for all uke players, including: Beauty and the Beast • Bibbidi-Bobbidi-Boo (The Magic Song) • Can You Feel the Love Tonight • Chim Chim Cher-ee • Heigh-Ho • It's a Small World • Some Day My Prince Will Come • We're All in This Together • When You Wish upon a Star • and more.

00701708 . . . .$14.99

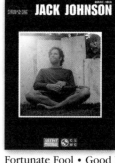

Jack Johnson – Strum & Sing

Cherry Lane Music
Strum along with 41 Jack Johnson songs using this top-notch collection of chords and lyrics just for the uke! Includes: Better Together • Bubble Toes • Cocoon • Do You Remember • Flake • Fortunate Fool • Good People • Holes to Heaven • Taylor • Tomorrow Morning • and more.

02501702 . . . .$17.99

The Beatles for Ukulele

Ukulele players can strum, sing and pick along with 20 Beatles classics! Includes: All You Need Is Love • Eight Days a Week • Good Day Sunshine • Here, There and Everywhere • Let It Be • Love Me Do • Penny Lane • Yesterday • and more.

00700154 . . . .$16.99

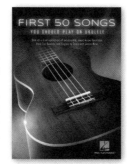

First 50 Songs You Should Play on Ukulele

An amazing collection of 50 accessible, must-know favorites: Edelweiss • Hey, Soul Sister • I Walk the Line • I'm Yours • Imagine • Over the Rainbow • Peaceful Easy Feeling • The Rainbow Connection • Riptide • and many more.

00149250 . . . .$14.99

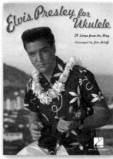

Elvis Presley for Ukulele

arr. Jim Beloff
20 classic hits from The King: All Shook Up • Blue Hawaii • Blue Suede Shoes • Can't Help Falling in Love • Don't • Heartbreak Hotel • Hound Dog • Jailhouse Rock • Love Me • Love Me Tender • Return to Sender • Suspicious Minds • Teddy Bear • and more.

00701004 . . . .$15.99

The Daily Ukulele

compiled and arranged by Liz and Jim Beloff
Strum a different song everyday with easy arrangements of 365 of your favorite songs in one big songbook! Includes favorites by the Beatles, Beach Boys, and Bob Dylan, folk songs, pop songs, kids' songs, Christmas carols, and Broadway and Hollywood tunes, all with a spiral binding for ease of use.

00240356 . . . .$39.99

Folk Songs for Ukulele

A great collection to take along to the campfire! 60 folk songs, including: Amazing Grace • Buffalo Gals • Camptown Races • For He's a Jolly Good Fellow • Good Night Ladies • Home on the Range • I've Been Working on the Railroad • Kumbaya • My Bonnie Lies over the Ocean • On Top of Old Smoky • Scarborough Fair • Swing Low, Sweet Chariot • Take Me Out to the Ball Game • Yankee Doodle • and more.

00696068 . . . .$12.99

Jake Shimabukuro – Peace Love Ukulele

Deemed "the Hendrix of the ukulele," Hawaii native Jake Shimabukuro is a uke virtuoso. Our songbook features note-for-note transcriptions with ukulele tablature of Jake's masterful playing on all the CD tracks: Bohemian Rhapsody • Boy Meets Girl • Bring Your Adz • Hallelujah • Pianoforte 2010 • Variation on a Dance 2010 • and more, plus two bonus selections!

00702516 . . . .$19.99

The Daily Ukulele – Leap Year Edition

366 More Songs for Better Living
compiled and arranged by Liz and Jim Beloff
An amazing second volume with 366 MORE songs for you to master each day of a leap year! Includes: Ain't No Sunshine • Calendar Girl • I Got You Babe • Lean on Me • Moondance • and many, many more.

00240681 . . . .$39.99

Hawaiian Songs for Ukulele

Over thirty songs from the state that made the ukulele famous, including: Beyond the Rainbow • Hanalei Moon • Ka-lu-a • Lovely Hula Girl • Mele Kalikimaka • One More Aloha • Sea Breeze • Tiny Bubbles • Waikiki • and more.

00696065 . . . .$10.99

Worship Songs for Ukulele

25 worship songs: Amazing Grace (My Chains are Gone) • Blessed Be Your Name • Enough • God of Wonders • Holy Is the Lord • How Great Is Our God • In Christ Alone • Love the Lord • Mighty to Save • Sing to the King • Step by Step • We Fall Down • and more.

00702546 . . . .$14.99

Disney characters and artwork © Disney Enterprises, Inc.

HAL•LEONARD®

Prices, contents, and availability subject to change.

0717